I Can Control My Anger

Written and Illustrated by
Dagmar Geisler

Translated by
Andrea Jones Berasaluce

Sky Pony Press
New York

First English translation copyright © 2019 by Skyhorse Publishing, Inc.

Published by arrangement with Loewe Verlag GmbH.
Title of the original German edition: *Wohin mit meiner wut?*
© 2017 Loewe Verlag GmhH, Bindlach

Sky Pony Press books may be purchased in bulk at special discounts for sales promotion, corporate gifts, fund-raising, or educational purposes. Special editions can also be created to specifications. For details, contact the Special Sales Department, Sky Pony Press, 307 West 36th Street, 11th Floor, New York, NY 10018 or info@skyhorsepublishing.com.

Sky Pony® is a registered trademark of Skyhorse Publishing, Inc.®, a Delaware corporation.

Visit our website at www.skyponypress.com.

10 9 8 7 6 5 4 3

Manufactured in China, June 2020
This product conforms to CPSIA 2008

Library of Congress Cataloging-in-Publication Data is available on file.

Cover provided by Loewe Verlag GmbH
Cover illustration by Dagmar Geisler

Print ISBN: 978-1-5107-4653-4
Ebook ISBN: 978-1-5107-4664-0

Dear Parents,

In everyday life, parents, educators, and teachers experience children becoming angry for a variety of reasons and demonstrating very different behaviors in response. If they unleash their feelings as a heavy outburst, it becomes a big challenge for all concerned.

Children keep hearing: "Stop being so angry!" "You're bad!" and "Pull yourself together!" But what are they supposed to do?

With this book, we want to invite you and your children into a complex and varied engagement with the subject: how does anger show itself and how can we express it without hurting anyone?

The lively and realistic images throughout encourage children to engage in an impartial dialogue and to think about their own behavior.

Children can strongly identify with the portrayals shown here and thus receive validation and affirmation to stand by their own personal feelings. Proven tips and tricks offer proposals and ideas that can help achieve a sense of calm.

This book also offers many approaches for educators concerned with strengthening emotional and social skills. By engaging in dialogue while reading the picture book, you can develop problem-solving steps individually or as a group.

With this complex topic, children need attention and guidance from us adults. With the help of this book, you can calmly look at stressful situations with your child "from the outside," and then together consider and agree upon changes that can be implemented.

Sabine von Bleichert,
Social Education Worker and Project Manager at echtstark.net

Do you
also get

angry

sometimes?

I do.

Sometimes I'm so angry, I want to scream loudly.

WAAAH!

I want to yell at somebody else.

I want to rip something up . . .

. . . or kick something.

Maybe I even want
to hit someone.

Crash

Boom . . .

Thwack . . .

When I'm angry,
my heart beats much faster than normal,
I get very hot, and my face turns red,
like a tomato.

Or I become very stiff,
and my face turns white as a sheet.
I get cold and clench my fists.

Sometimes, the anger creeps in very slowly.

At first, it's just a little annoyance, but then it will get worse and worse, until I'm really angry.

Other times I get angry so quickly, I scare myself.

If someone asks why I'm angry, I usually know exactly why.

I get angry if someone takes something from me.

Or when I get laughed at, or when someone is mean to me.

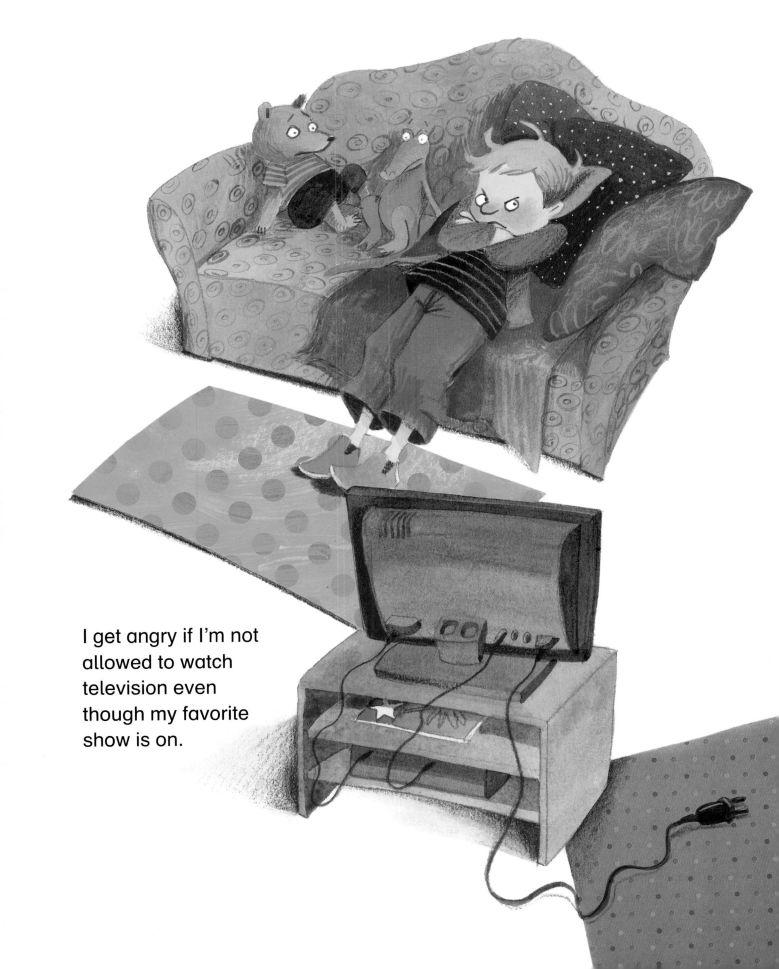

I get angry if I'm not allowed to watch television even though my favorite show is on.

Sometimes I get angry, too, when someone breaks something of mine.

And if something goes wrong for me, I can also get pretty sour.

But sometimes I'm extremely angry and don't know why.

This is a stupid feeling. And because it's a stupid feeling, I get even *more* angry.

When someone tells me, "Don't be so angry!", it doesn't make things better. I'm still angry. Nobody's at fault, yet I want to smack someone.

But that would be totally wrong, right?

What am I supposed to do then when I'm sooo angry?

Luckily, I know a few tricks:

I can shout my anger
out the window.

I can beat
up a thick
pillow.

I can stomp the anger deep
into the ground.

I can draw angry figures and tear the
sheet into a thousand small pieces.

I can bury my stupid
rage in the garden.

I can ball up papers with my anger and throw them as far as I can.

That doesn't hurt anyone.

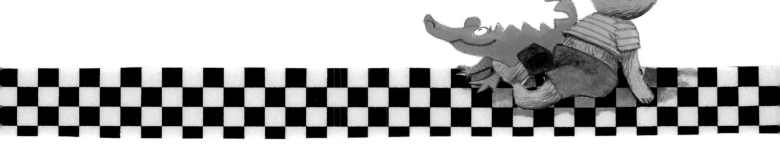

Phew!

And above all, I can first
take a deep breath.

But if I do throw a fit, I can at least say I'm sorry.

And if I have a reason for my anger, because someone really did something to me?

Should I yell at them?
Or hit or kick them?

I'd rather not! I don't like it at all when anyone yells at me—it scares me.

And if someone kicks or pinches me, it hurts.

But I can say, loudly:

"Leave me alone!"

Or: "Give that back! It's mine!"

Or I can say:

"Please, don't forbid me from watching my favorite show."

And what if someone else is angry?

What if they're much bigger and stronger than me and aren't stopping at all?

What do I do then?

I could say, for example:

"Stop! Take a deep breath first!"

And when he has taken a deep breath,
I can reveal to him all my good tricks.

Maybe he doesn't know them yet.

But if that doesn't work,
we can go get help.

And that's okay! Sometimes we are angry.

But most of the time, we are actually quite nice.